The Lengest Neoi

Winner of the Iowa Poetry Prize

The
Lengest
Neoi

BY

STEPHANIE

CHOI

University of Iowa Press, Iowa City

University of Iowa Press, Iowa City 52242
Copyright © 2024 by Stephanie Choi
uipress.uiowa.edu
Printed in the United States of America

Cover design by Susan Zucker
Text design and typesetting by Ashley Muehlbauer

Printed on acid-free paper

Library of Congress Cataloging-in-Publication Data
Names: Choi, Stephanie, author.
Title: The Lengest Neoi / Stephanie Choi.
Description: Iowa City: University of Iowa Press,
2024. | Series: Iowa Poetry Prize
Identifiers: LCCN 2023036724 (print) | LCCN
2023036725 (ebook) | ISBN 9781609389512 (paperback;
acid-free paper) | ISBN 9781609389529 (ebook)
Subjects: LCGFT: Poetry.
Classification: LCC PS3603.H6547 L46 2024 (print)
| LCC PS3603.H6547 (ebook) | DDC 811/.6—dc23/
eng/20231020
LC record available at https://lccn.loc.gov/2023036724
LC ebook record available at https://lccn.loc.gov
/2023036725

for my parents
and grandparents

Contents

So Many Wet Feet Everywhere

the world's lunch spilled. on soaked streets with sewer steam rising
popping corn on a gas stove. i was listening. i was always
listening. following ounces until blues blurred. until my body
caught in cracks of RTA track. somewhere between doing laundry
and growing bitter gourd grandma said we were poor.
i map out emission reduction goals & find
in a new infrastructure improvement plan
rails of her skeleton. of all her hands papered.
just a hundred years memory of erased past.
i set my tear-soaked bread in the sun to dry
wives of white men tell me: this is what will make it rise.
there's warm and warm enough & i'm supposed to know
which is right for my body in the burning bread cavity.
i search the back of every back bedroom dresser
for socks. it's all my time spent searching for socks
semi-clean. somewhat similar. at least enough
for my feet standing in at the bus stop seeing
all that's walking on in the near dark of natural light.

To Error in Translation

I.

An elephant on the road bisecting rows of puri stands; behind them, sunset on sari-filled storefront windows. I walked behind someone following someone else following someone else following our hostel tour guide. Single file, stopping only to take pictures of the elephant, touch saris, and eat puri. The pink city as it's called: Jaipur. From Mumbai, it was the longest train ride I had ever been on—overnight, 22 hours. A young girl shared a lower berth with me. Only sweat and sweet monsoon air between us. Halfway through the night she opened her palm before me, revealing her array of orange snacks—clementines, cheese-covered chips, candies. She didn't want to sleep. She said what English words she knew; asked me how old I was, told me she was eight. At dawn, as was customary, someone opened the train doors for fresh air; I had come to love standing at the doorway—the wind against my face, never seeing any one thing for more than a second while looking out in any direction. The girl's stop was several before Jaipur; she said *goodbye*, that they were going to *see grandma*. My gaze followed her as she walked through the station's crowd turned sideways toward me, waving with her left hand, her right hand holding her mother's—their interwoven fingers kaleidoscoping into air as the train pulled away.

II.

My grandmother gave me my Chinese name. I carried the characters written on a scrap of envelope around as a photo on my phone. At a club, that first night in Jaipur, I asked a boy from Hong Kong to translate the characters. Translating them didn't make them mean anything.

III.

There's the other name—*pretty girl*—who can be anyone: a granddaughter, shopkeeper, waitress, cousin. My other name I've tried to adorn since I was born. My other name my grandmother says, her hand on my cheek. To be a pretty girl.

Leng lui is formal; leng neoi is how you write it for someone learning to speak it, the boy from Hong Kong told me, *people would be able to understand.*

I make her superlative—the lengest: the tongue writing herself, learning to speak.

A Voicemail from Grandma: When I Did Not Return

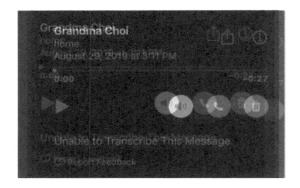

I.

(to error in transcription) *

auhh . . . uh noi uh . . . nay han gaw naw guah wah . . . naw hy ning ning uh . . . muh nay
ewuh nay uh . . . ning ning cah nay mo haa uh . . . yea . . . mommy yuh cah nay wah . . . nay
fye fan uh gay gun ning ning aye . . . nay ewuh nay uh . . . auhh . . . nay yuh han gow uh noi
mow . . . ning ning cay nay m foon wah . . .

consulting your lover's salt-glistening skin, surfing a wave in the South China Sea

II.

(to error in transliteration) *

néiu . . . néih tèng ngóh dihn wá . . . ngóh haih ngin ngin . . . néih heui bīn . . . ngin ngin
dàam sàm tai néih mh-hou . . . yeah . . . mommy dàam sàm tai néih . . . néih faai fàan-heui
ngūk-kéi gin ngin ngin . . . néih heui bīn . . . néih yiu hàhng gòu néiu móuh . . . ngin ngin
dàam sàm tai néih mh fan . . .

consulting your Cantonese, Parker Po-fei Huang's Cantonese Dictionary, *and a photograph of her
bitter gourd growing in mismatched pots along a chain-link fence*

III.

(to error in translation) *

(sigh). . . granddaughter . . . do you hear my phone call . . . this is grandma . . . where are you . . . grandma worries about you do not do this . . . yeah . . . mommy worries about you . . . you hurry and come home by grandma . . . where are you . . . (sigh) . . . you need to be good, innocent granddaughter, grandma worries about you and can't sleep . . .

consulting half a custard apple a stranger offered you on a bus from Manila to La Union

IV.

(to error in translation) *

(sigh) . . . granddaughter . . . do you hear my phone call . . . this is grandma . . . where have you gone to . . . I am afraid for you I'm not happy . . . yeah . . . mommy is afraid for you . . . you hurry and return home and visit grandma . . . where have you gone to . . . (sigh) . . . you want to behave, innocent granddaughter, grandma worries about you and does not sleep . . .

consulting maple leaves crushed underneath your feet

V.

(to error in translation) *

(sigh) . . . granddaughter . . . can you receive my phone call . . . this is grandma . . . where have you gone to . . . I am afraid for you I'm not eating . . . yeah . . . mommy is afraid for you . . . you hurry and return home and join grandma . . . where have you gone to . . . (sigh) . . . you must be good, granddaughter, grandma worries about you and can't sleep . . .

consulting a dab of Tiger Balm spread on a bruise

VI.

(to error in translation) *

(sigh) . . . granddaughter . . . can you hear my phone call . . . this is grandma . . . where have you gone to . . . I am afraid for you don't do this . . . yeah . . . mommy is afraid for you . . . you hurry and return home and be with grandma . . . where have you gone to . . . (distressed sigh) . . . you must behave with principle, innocent granddaughter, grandma worries about you and does not sleep . . .

consulting an old jam jar filled with cactus spines

Spine / Vine

The pain persists as a pinch
        where spine curves into shoulder-
                blade pressed — knots — sore
                        no stretch stretches out

this edge — sharp — sharpening

        can't for a moment forget
                years ago treatment, a brace
                        around my whole torso
                                shell I shed

named diagnosis, genetic predisposition

        remains, my grandmother
                hunchbacked tending bitter gourd
                        in her backyard, her body
                                within mine, a vine

I'd lose too
if I wished the pain away

A Last Name That Fell from the Sky

I.

蔡 flown across the Pacific in 1969, my father took his first steps in America with a new last name the same year an American man took his first steps on the moon. Romanized based on the Cantonese pronunciation, 蔡 became Choi on immigration papers; could have been Tsoi, Tsai, Chai, Cai, or Toi—which is what my mother told me was the real last name— why it was changed, I can never remember the story. Maybe there's no elaborate story— simply how the immigration officer heard the name off my grandfather's tongue. He's been dead five years now and I can't recall ever hearing him say our last name. My grandmother placed a journal and a pen in his coffin at the wake. I imagine him writing to her; though, as far as I know, she cannot read or write. I cannot say 蔡 in the correct tone.

II.

My father likes to tell me how at his high school graduation, there was a whole row of Chois, Chas, Chows, Chos, and Chous—even the teachers announcing them were amused saying one name after another. For years I cringed during attendance, waiting for the teacher to say Chow or Cho or Chou. Now, I cringe when people ask me if I'm Korean— they insist, my last name *is Korean*; or, when the bookstore owner in Massachusetts glances too long at my credit card and asks if Choi is a popular last name because he happens to know several authors with that last name.

III.

My internet research tells me 蔡 (Cài) derives from the name of the ancient Cài state. It's the 38th most common surname in China, 9th in Taiwan, and 8th in Singapore. For each dialect, each language spoken, a different romanization. Cài is 채 in Hangul, pronounced Chae. In Vietnamese, Thái, sometimes Sái. We're all said to be the descendants of the 5th son of King Wen of Zhou, who fathered 10 sons with his wife and at least another 8 with concubines. There's much praise for him in the *Shih Ching*—the oldest existing collection of Chinese poetry; it's on my reading list. To be in the lineage of a king, of a legitimate son— how lucky—I suppose it's how we've thrived.

IV.

There'll always be a screen between me and my ancestry. I can only follow the "i" moving—蔡, two eyes looking from Cài to Choi to I.

Portrait of Louisa Cobb Thompson
by an Unidentified Chinese Artist
at the Nantucket Whaling Museum

She's twice made, an image:
first ambrotype, then painting
side by side behind the glass display,
part of Nantucket & the World—

she's the wife of the Captain,
of the last Nantucket whaler,
and was dead when he sailed
across far seas, a photograph of her

in his pocket. Somewhere,
he met a Chinese artist
who must have agreed to paint
her for cheap (at least in dollars).

He mirrored the photograph
so that in the painting I see
her left arm instead of right
slightly bent, resting gently

on her dress, which he guessed
was black, though it might
have been brown or blue.
He kept her lace collar white,

but made the collar button
red—for her earrings and lips
too. He wanted to give her
some luck, vitality, happiness,

all held in a color—or maybe
he saw it in her photograph, in her—
who knows if he knew she was dead.
The didactic merely says:

—The porcelain complexion
and Asiatic appearance of the eyes
gives this painting away
as the work of a Chinese artist—

So I make up any history
through looking—at her, at his
painting. I take my own
photo of her on my phone,

now a third image—mine
to remember what I want:
that red—that red I identify
by—my ancestor's hand.

My Name

for Marilyn Chin

Watching tennis in '95, Mom found my name.
Its roots in Greek—crowned—my name.

Not another with the same until 10th grade calculus—
used the ∫ for "S" so there was no confusion around my name.

A Chinese one too given at birth. Mom says,
You have to ask your grandmother about that name.

Always wanted to be after a season, flower, river, bird, or
at least with a better story. Wanted something beautiful to expound on my name.

My teammates, my mom on the bleachers—all those swim meets
racing the 100 fly. The cheering—*go, go!*—drowned my name.

Grandpa could never say it, called me *Jeffany, Jeffanyuh*—
mother tongue cannot pronounce the *st, st* sound in my name.

Every now and then I burn my papers—to-do lists, poems, letters
I never sent. I bury the ashes in the ground—my name.

That which we call a rose by any other name would smell
as sweet . . . Lilac, Tulip, Daffodil—I point, say aloud each name.

The characters she chose for me: beautiful, wild wave—my grandmother
made her former surname her American name, Mi—surrounds my name.

The weight of the crown, the water on my skin. Each word
I write is mine—*Stephanie's*—bound to my name.

Speech Derapy

for Li-Young Lee

Dey discovered it in dird grade
whenever we practiced counting
money, candy, or some oder ding
I kept saying *dirty, dirty*—

*say thirty, thirty—see how
she cannot pronounce th, th*
de teacher said to my parents.

In de car on de way home
mom said to dad, *you
pronounce things like that
sometimes, she probably
gets it from you.*

After dat, a lady came
dree times a week
to pull me out
of independent reading.

I can't remember
the other kids being cruel,
laughing at me—
each time I left, each time
I said *dird or dirty or de*—

though it might be easier
to write this poem
about that, I only remember

de small room filled
with games we played,
memory, go fish, bingo.

I practiced following
de lady's mouth,
pushing my tongue
into my front teeth
again and again
until I could say it—

thirty, I smiled
at mom, proud
that I could match
her *good* English—

she practiced as a child
to pay bills, navigate
the bus and grocery store
for her parents—

proud to discover
dat I might be able
to fix any ding
in myself.

My Last Tattoo

i.

The white blossoms now nearly invisible. Ink that's faded, or never quite took. I was supposed to return for touch-ups after six months, but by then I was already back in America.

I didn't know I'd have returned at the time, reclined in the plush leather chair, my left arm laid relaxed—the drone of the tattoo gun more numbing than the needles themselves.

ii.

My sister-in-law recommended the place, in her hometown, Saigon, where I was staying with her family as I passed through, wandering across Asia. She wasn't my sister-in-law then, just my brother's girlfriend, home for the summer.

iii.

Hours before, we walked the floors of the War Remnants Museum, avoided lingering too long in front of any one piece, looking too closely. We said nothing to each other as we snaked around each room. Remnants, I remember thinking, was a good word.

iv.

The year Saigon fell, my parents—new Americans, first generation—just children learning English as a second language. Their old country's power defeating their new country's power in a country they'd never been to, probably couldn't yet point to on a map.

I, then, a remnant—a Chinese American traveling, carefree—far enough removed from history, yet close enough to get a visa on arrival.

v.

It represents home, I said to the artist as he pulled lines of green up my bicep, curving them to make the arms of the saguaro. It was so important to me then, on the other side of the world, to have that—an indelible image of home; maybe, even more, my imagined meaning of it. The desert, the place I'd grown up only half my life, but whose vistas I took within me.

vi.

First named the Exhibition House for US and Puppet Crimes, then changed in 1990 to the Exhibition House for Crimes of War and Aggression, then again in 1995—the year of my birth— to the War Remnants Museum.

vii.

My sister-in-law's father planned a week-long family vacation in Da Nang. We stayed in a house on the beach, went on a river boat tour where they gave us straw hats to wear, and ate at a resort brunch buffet each morning.

We waited hours to walk across the Golden Bridge, to be upheld by giant hands suspended in sky; and sat for hours in the evening, watching the Dragon Bridge spit fire.

viii.

The saguaro cactus, native to the place in a way I wasn't; and yet, there I was, claiming it— exposing my American-ness. In my imagination: *my home, to be from.* In my imagination, I am at least some part colonizer. I am at least some part colonizer.

ix.

Shortly after I got the tattoo, my mother noticed an edge of it peeking out from my t-shirt sleeve in a photo I sent her; the first one she ever saw—my last one.

x.

I don't go to the North, my sister-in-law said. I didn't either while I was there. Fellow travelers told me to ride the Chinese border on motorbike. *An incredible experience,* they swooned.

xi.

I wanted to wear an image of home, but I didn't want to go home. I wanted to be as far away from America as possible. It was 2018. *You should go home, your parents miss you,* my sister-in-law said. Still, she helped me search for English teaching jobs.

xii.

My first tattoo I got when I was sixteen with my best friend at the time. She was one of the only other Asian girls at my high school.

When after ten years of friendship I felt my connection with her fading, I stopped responding to her text messages, answering her calls. I never told her about my long trip abroad, all the places I went to in Vietnam, where her family was from.

She still wishes me Happy Birthday.

xiii.

Eventually, I bought a return ticket.

xiv.

I hardly look at the tattoos on my body anymore; sometimes I even forget I have them, surprised when I catch a glimpse in the mirror, coming out of the shower or putting on a summer dress.

Spinebound

Spine grew crooked
Spine fit into a brace
Spine still crooked

Open Wide

small mouth with too many teeth   the dentist making small talk
over the buzzing   eight extracted before age ten   easier each time
                    shot of novocaine came

I closed my eyes   against overhead lights   to learn that pain might be
          rewarded: a free frosty at Wendy's   a pink plastic treasure chest   the width
                                                            of a hard candy
                    with my baby teeth inside

Trace Asymmetries

I.

You can feel it for yourself

        & my mother did
                placed her index finger & thumb
on the tip of my chin
                slid them back over my jawline
(light blue bib around my neck)
        as the dentist had,
        tracing

feel how the right side _____

        she nodded
                moved her thumb
        along the _____

she has too many _____*, has* _____
        shouldn't need surgery if we _____ *,* _____ *,* _____

        they did
and I can feel the _____ still
        my palm on my chin
                two fingers
        tracing,
                back

II.

You can feel it for yourself

        & my mother did
                placed middle and index fingers
at the nape of my neck
                ran them down my spine
(light blue gown over my body)
        as the doctor had,
        tracing

feel how it _____

        she nodded
                fingers running
        over the _____

she has _____
        shouldn't need surgery if we _____

        they did
and I can feel the _____ still
                my hand on my spine
                    two fingers
        tracing,

Autumn Thoughts

A piece of paper atop
      one leaf placed vein up
            rubbed crayon impression

Tomato plants topple over
      each other and their cages
            wire entangled roots

A blue-gray chill haunts
      the horizon, a quartet
            of crows fly silent

The sparrow has no place to perch
      sunflower heads hang, necks broken
            no treat in grapes, all gone

Violet smears across sidewalk signal
      what was, what will be
            erased in snow

Shovels set out on porches
      my footsteps precede me
            on sun-lit curbs of streets

Across the meadow—
      only a chickadee's echo
            am I even here?

The Leng³est Neoi⁵⁻²

in the beginning / leng neoi / is the lengest / leng neoi / will ever be / be what / the waitress / at dim sum / is summoned by / be miss / chinatown / miss chinatown / praised as / what's called out / to foreign / white women / in hong kong / leng-est / they are / I am / I'm made / I've made / some kind / of chinglish / ching-lish / the asian / jess day / he said / I was like / at the party / my friend / took me to / I was wearing / my flower dress / my cat socks / they were / christmas-themed / themed / oriental party / at the / fraternity house / a headline / somewhere / somewhere / a white woman / wearing / a cheap / cheongsam / bought / at some / vintage / boutique / a leng neoi / needed money / money given / in a red envelope / to leng neoi / at birth / in the beginning / leng neoi / comes out / of the womb / already a wound

---

3. flat mid

5-2. high flat; low falling

Diaspora

a sound translation after Jonathan Stalling

mulberry-stained finger
        mòuh lìu báau yi-si tai doih fan gaau

empty-handed, full meaning in place of sleep:
        yìm tái hahn deih fú la mehng pài làai séi pa

salt look, desire land, bitter rift. life whittles. drag death, fear
        sai lāt sì yìh láan daaih biu táih fāt láih féi wai tài daaih gā deui fuh fā yeh

young. off down region, suspect orchid headlines, remove decorum, fat feed.
        watch all of us handle flower night.

The Key

I'd need it all
eventually,
a retainer for life
braces, twice
but first headgear
an expander
to go with it

to make space
in my mouth
too small
to pull back
my jaw, under-
bite crooked

each night mom
fit the key
into the metal
screwed
onto the roof
of my mouth
and turned
three times

each day my mouth
was widening
if only the width
between two teeth

every day
a little pain
tightness
constraint
I stopped
wincing at

each twist
of her wrist
in my mouth
she said *sorry,*
sorry

she didn't know
she was turning
the song
right out of me

On Cacti

Those needles
also known as
spines

Lipogram

This poem will not be a lipogram.

The following sentence will try to explain what happened without the letter *e*:

In my youth I got a tattoo with a word that's missing an __.

This poem is not inspired by the novel *Gadsby*, whose cover touts it as a 50,000-word novel without the letter *e*.

This poem is not inspired by the book *La Disparition*, inspired by the book *Gadsby*.

This poem is not inspired.

What happened is that when I was twenty I got a tattoo from a guy my friend met at a club.

What happened is that my friend met a guy at a club who said he *did tattoos* and exchanged Snapchats with him.

What happened is that we tapped through his artist portfolio, made up of photos that disappeared after 5 seconds.

What happened is that my friend wanted a pinecone and I wanted a tree with some lines from a poem I loved.

What happened is that he quoted us a quarter of studio prices and arrived at her house with his toolbox full of needles and ink.

What happened is that I was twenty.

What happened is that he plastic-wrapped the kitchen table and for three hours I clutched my friend's couch pillow.

What happened is that he misspelled the word _____.

What happened is that he said *sometimes it can be painful on the* back . . . over *the spine*.

What happened is that I already knew pain in my spine.

What happened is a childhood diagnosis, an adolescent correction.

What happened is that I wore a back brace and then I didn't.

What happened is that I hid the brace under a revolving trove of various large, plain colored T-shirts I made my mother buy for me from the craft store.

What happened made invisible.

What happened is that when I stopped wearing the brace the pain remained.

What happened is that the pain from the needles would at least leave something visible.

What happened is that because *e* is the most common letter, it's often mis-seen—the eye places it there, where it is not.

What happened is that I mis-saw.

What happened is that it was not an intentional omission of the letter *e*, but a mistake.

What happened is that a friend finally noticed and said *I'm so sorry to tell you this*.

What happened is that the word *loneliness* is missing its first *e*.

What happened is that I took it as a sign.

What happened is that I was twenty and desired *meaning*.

What happened is that the word loneliness went from long to short *O*.

What happened is that the tattoo is on my back, which means I never see it.

What happened is that the tattoo is on my back, which means I always see it:

A tattoo with a word missing an __, and I with a story.

Two-Winged Sunset in Penang

I am the remnants of this:
shades of fuchsia adventure turned dim.
Only the gold essence
of another self, long left.

I lost my earrings once.
They were fuchsia and gold rimmed.
Fell onto a dance floor in Penang—
where a part of myself had been shed.

American | Ghost | Chestnut

lose leaves branches bark let the wind
fill what's still here stumps of once seminal
trees once forest now what skeletal
remains are left are left for scientists'
play citizen nostalgia *good old days*
harvesting nuts   sawing timber
no longer mighty giants instead
functionally extinct 4 billion felled
from maine to georgia in 40 years
in 1914, haven metcalf writes
it is too late to exclude this undesirable
citizen: but we can at least redouble
our efforts to see that no others
get a foothold on this continent

to see that no others get a foothold
pass the page act 1875 station agents
to ask any woman arriving from china,
japan, or any oriental country if they
are here by voluntary consent
hear no before it is said see only
sin *importation for the purpose of*
prostitution shall be held guilty
decades before two brothers imported
afong moy as a _____ exhibited
alongside chinese objects to entice buyers
bound feet the women held in cells
line up for inspection search eyes nose mouth
still the source of infection is unknown

still the source of infection is unknown
destruction persists dead and dying trees
a blight first noted in 1904 the bronx zoo
disease that girdles the tree study proceeds
the most common way the fungus enters
through wounds as in a boy carved a heart
the initials of his lover into bark a pathway
suddenly for the pathogen   across
all 250 acres of the zoo   founded
only a few years before   a place
for conservation   by conservationists
like madison grant   who leads efforts
for eugenics   writes *the passing*
of the great race   inspires _____

the great race _____ inspires
makes permanent chinese exclusion 1904
emergence of japan as imperial power 1904
franz boas organizes largest human zoo 1904
in history thousands bought and exhibited 1904
in reconstructions of native habitats 1904
in st louis and then for some time after 1904
bodies transported to the bronx zoo where 1904
grant oversaw the cages amongst dying
trees noted blight a fungus a disease
found to exist in new jersey, maryland . . .
_____ cut off circulation
not enough time to save them
spores spread quick over long distances

diasporic   body of people spread
my grandmother returns after 40 years
packs a suitcase of photos   to show
aunts uncles cousins   in the village
i meet for the first time the ones who
didn't get sponsored   i ask why
_____ she says   hands out
red envelopes filled with _____
bamboo persimmon plum   forty-two
varieties of soybean   frank n. meyer
plant explorer took   searching for
evidence of the blight in china he
returned with samples and new seeds
promptly planted in american soil

planted in american soil   gold
so came the chinese   claim to mine
and find neither wealth nor welcome
though the treaties were signed naming
china *the most favored nation for trade*
low-cost labor   gold turned to railroad
so more came still   staked their skeletons
in western landscapes   dad and i drive
through   he says we probably have a relative
buried here somewhere   we don't know
why my research on chestnuts matters
i can't say   what i see in the trees
where my interest began traced back
to a white man mistracing the origin of blight

origin of the blight   a white man tells me
it was imported   on chinese chestnuts
mis spoke mis named mis remembered
japanese chestnuts first shipped on accident
in a pack of lily bulbs to s. b. parsons
of flushing he planted them delighted
when they grew a new variety of the beloved
nut   larger but not as sweet   as the american
the chinese were found to be laborious
but unable to assimilate   *a chinaman is*
a chinaman wherever he goes   and go
he went   *removal is highly desirable* written
in newspapers   word of the blight began
tree enemies infest america, says grower

trees growing in china were resistant
meyer reported though the blight was
evident there seemed to be no effect
on the asian species a fungus evolved
mutually with there was no remedy
for the americans   efforts directed
toward salvaging the timber that could
be cut down millions of trees left
stumps still the blight attacking only
bodies not roots new shoots grew
only to die again and again but hope
too grew an idea of resilience an idea
to crossbreed the two for resistance
to this day still trying to bring back life

to this day still trying to bring back life
valiant efforts to restore american chestnuts
no longer a vital food or lumber source
so it's not about necessity but nostalgia
and they say as much *a culture a* _____
_____ they say   the american chestnut
foundation its members fervent researchers
petitioning the usda to allow distribution
of their transgenic chestnut more resistant
than those backcross bred opposition
from indigenous tribes activists who say
the effects of introducing a gmo into the forest
is dangerous   human caused   destruction
precedent   unknown consequences

X-bred

Across

3. the hands that make
5. carried
7. a culture no longer
9. of origin
10. like skin
12. want to rid of
13. finds a way in
15. a measure of distances between
16. bones of the west's railroads

Down

1. to cross
2. planted
4. to replace with
6. distinct but related
8. entangled
10. infected
11. their coming
14. a force against which

unknown consequences precedent
under occupation my grandparents were born
war time famine japan's intent to rule
all of asia made them enemy of the states
and china a sudden ally the exclusion act lifted
pearl harbor bombed japanese interned
my grandfather's medals on my mother's altar
chinese he fought for america a paper son
he died when i was in kindergarten the teacher
gave us a piece of paper with a person's outline
and told us to fill the person in with *what you are*
ask your parents and i did and the next day
when i saw everyone else's person divided up
i changed mine split her in half *chinese japanese*

japanese chinese whatever i am decided
by whomever i'm in front of   a cashier
a cab driver a man walking in a crosswalk
bowing to me as he passes   whispering
ni hao   until i look   *but your eyes*
are so big she said when i told her
i was _____ both of us in line
for the asian sorority info session
i never joined   instead found kinship
amongst trees joining every outdoors
environmental club i could where i learned
to compost hike garden i grew bitter gourd
my grandmother's saved seeds and styrofoam
takeout boxes her own *sustainability*

not in any book   her own *sustainability*
from *ten*   to stretch   *sustinere* to hold up
endure nearly ninety though we don't know
her exact date of birth she signs her name
Mi the only word she knows how to write
in english or chinese   illiterate defined
in the language she refused to learn to speak
i'll never know why   never be able to ask
on the phone with her i realize i'm losing
more and more   of my ability to comprehend
even when i know what she will say
did you eat   don't go outside   when are you
coming   i dread   picking up a reminder
of how distant i've grown from my own roots

how distant the crossbred transgenic
chestnuts are from the original american
scientists society desires to preserve
the iconic traits of the tree tall and straight
growing   unlike the asian varieties which
grow more outward dwarfed orchard-like
ornamental   and the nuts not as sweet
i remember the red plastic mesh bags
piled in cardboard boxes at the ends
of produce aisles at ranch 99 dad
wok-roasted them childhood christmases
peeled the skin back for me yellow flesh
i sat at the counter eating   innocent
still of the histories that defined me

still of the histories that define me
exclusion peril conflation with a thing
or another person my mother stopped
on the sidewalk a man telling her she
looks just like _____ my grandmother's
soup will be lost when she goes no one
learned how to make the zong either
and a way of life will be lost i know
a way of life was lost when the chestnut went
coal came now abandoned mines stripped
land that scientists hope gmo chestnuts
will restore in the photo a white hand
pollinates the tree the fungus both me i
lose i make myself language bones skin

leaves branches bark lost let the wind
see that no others get a foothold
still the source of infection is unknown
the great race _____ inspires
diasporic   body of people spread
planted in american soil   gold
origin of the blight   a white man tells me
trees growing in china were resistant
to this day still trying to bring back life
unknown consequences precedent
japanese chinese whatever i am decided
not in any book   her own sustainability
how distant the crossbred transgenic
still of the histories that define me

////

When I Watched *In the Mood for Love* at a Bar in Ipoh, Malaysia
for Wong Kar-wai

[1]

It was my first time, a fact I'm embarrassed to admit as I was 23. Across the alleyway from my hostel, where I was the only guest, a hidden bar—backlit exposed brick like I was in Brooklyn. The light switched off to screen the movie, whiskey and gin bottles silhouetted the bottom sixth of the frame.

No subtitles. *This is a classic*, my bar neighbor, Louisa, said. She was not from Ipoh, but somewhere else in Malaysia. I don't remember where. Her name in my phone saved: "Luisa Tiga Bar Ipoh."

[2]

Not translation, but narration: *They're neighbors and their spouses are cheating with each other, but they don't know it yet,* Louisa chuckled. Between her narration and my kindergarten comprehension of Cantonese, I followed the plot—my attention turned on particular shots—

[3]

Shadows against an alleyway cement wall

      Shoulders brushing past one another
            down the stairwell to the noodle stall

Narrow meetings in doorways, the apartment hall

[4]

It was my third consecutive night at the bar, arriving alone to sip some tamarind, pandan, or lemongrass infused drink. I journaled the other nights about some man, a local, I'd spent one night with in Indonesia a month before. In a few days, I'd return to try to find him.

[5]

A handbag, a tie; *this is when they figure it out. Coincidences,* Louisa said, giggling. Of course, it's funny because it is no coincidence Chow's wife has the same handbag as Su and Su's husband has the same tie as Chow.

[6]

Cut red meat in a red diner booth, red carpet floor

      Skin-tight cheongsam, light blue with red flowers

         Red curtains sweep the length of a corridor

[7]

I imagined we would meet again in the same place. I'd wrap my arms around his waist on the back of his motorbike as we swerved down crowded roads—a solitary blur.

[8]

They don't want to be like their spouses, they just want to pretend—reenact.

      One palm grazes another,
           long taxi rides alone together

What's real and what's pretend? I can't tell without translation. Louisa's narration becomes sparser, and looser with every next cocktail.

[9]

Never having been a smoker in America, I took to it while traveling, fidgeting each Esse Slim between my fingers like a pen.

[10]

The camera keeps returning to a large Siemens clock hanging in Su's office.

[11]

That one night we spent together, I showed him some of the lines in my journal. He asked me what a lawnmower was, pointed to a line he said he loved: *I met a stranger yesterday. He's a stranger today.*

[12]

I've re-watched the movie a handful of times now (with subtitles); I've never tried to read the time on the clock.

It's not about time, but timing—

[13]

Sand tracks in, settles between white tile cracks

      My sandal in the living room, I never get back

The strap chewed off—his dogs—in my head, their bark

[14]

Louisa was my mother's age. She sent me her facebook page: *Louisa's Mandala Art & Numerology*. Like me, she was traveling alone. *Here in Malaysia, everyone speaks five languages,* she said.

I didn't know Cantonese was one of them before I arrived. I tried to order an egg tart— words I knew, the few I could speak with my grandmother. The cashier laughed at me.

[15]

I returned to Indonesia but did not meet him again. Maybe I felt something like Su when she arrives at Chow's apartment in Singapore, calls him at work from his own phone and rests it on her shoulder, unable to speak as Chow repeats *Hello*.

[16]

She leaves a lipsticked butt of a cigarette in his ashtray.

[17]

I left the bar before the movie ended. Louisa was preoccupied, chatting in Hakka with the bartender. Now, when I click Louisa's facebook page it says *the link you followed may be broken, or the page may have been removed.*

[18]

Years later, Chow presses his face into a stone hollow of Angkor Wat. What he says cannot be translated. He fills the hollow with earth.

[19]

I searched for hours for the journal where I wrote about watching *In the Mood for Love* for the first time at a bar in Ipoh, Malaysia. I wanted to get the details right, but the journal has been misplaced.

Poem Written in My Grandmother's Dress

Rust orange and brown checkered,
thick but not quite wool. Not quite

cotton either though I can't name it,
can't identify it on the internet.

So I resign, run my fingers along the hem,
try to hear the song she sang into each seam—

guess how many times she slipped it over
her dyed black and permed hair, lotioned

white face. I estimate the exact place
it might have fallen over her panty-hosed

covered knees. This is real *vintage*—
from my grandmother's closet,

and yet, I can't even ask her about it.
I couldn't ask for it then either—

My mother translated. My grandmother
smiled, pulled it out quickly and put it into

my arms. Gently, I held each end over
my head and slipped myself underneath.

She placed her palm on the small of my back
and said, *hou leng, hou leng* to my

reflection in the mirror. Of course, I fit
her dress the way I never will her tongue.

The dream was not about missing a train

but missing. This morning house finches
sing perched along the telephone line.
I stand so far apart from you that when
I reach to brush my hair I am brushing yours.

To Write One's Name

Cài
蔡
Family Name

I.

table with three legs
drapes flowing down

each side, a trellis
for gourd vine

II.

place to serve ancestors
bitter gourd

eyes bow toward
birds and sky

Lì
麗
Beautiful

I.

almost symmetry
extra line on the left side

my back, a curved spine
through square windows

II.

a face above
crooked body

peering out
to garden of gourds

Tāo
濤
Wild Wave

I.

two arms and a leg
trying to escape

pressure of lines
stacked horizontal

II.

unbearable weight
on a seat and desk

rooting
a wild wave

Emails from Mom

I.

Subject: Do not meet strangers to purchase items. Buy from a store. Do not risk it!

Body: https://www.msn.com/en-us/news/crime/colo-parents-of-5-killed-while-trying-to-buy-used-car-were-most-loving-people-ever-says-sister/ar-BB18PIqO?ocid=mailsignout

RE:

Many nights I've spent on my phone scrolling facebook
marketplace, buy nothing, free & for sale. The account
I made just for this: a duck lamp, red-framed mirror, instant
pot, bookshelf, polaroid camera. A bicycle in each new city
I moved to. Drove to houses, parking lots, requested delivery
for things I could haggle for—the way grandma taught me
caressing scarves and jade with one hand, the other holding mine.

II.

Subject: FW: Do These Things Cause Cancer?

Body: Use the speaker if you talk on your cell phone. Do not keep it near your body.

RE:

Held it to my ear the last time we spoke. You and dad
were flying somewhere that night. *Let me just remind you*
the password to the safe, and dad has some coins stored
behind your dollhouse. You have always been paranoid,
superstitious, absorbed in the news—a plane crashed
somewhere in China yesterday, and you are making sure

I live well into tomorrow. Even if I'm not. Even when
I sleep with my phone under the pillow, get tattoos
at bars in other countries, swim in the sea at midnight
for lovers, walk new cities without pepper spray, and cross roads
without looking both ways. You birthed me, so you must.

Before We Summit Mt. Washington

July 2020

Evening at the campsite, children run past us, whisper
chinese people, chinese people, chinese people . . .
giggle, reach the playground, swing and slide.
I don't turn my head; I'm not sure you hear

chinese people, chinese people, chinese people—
you are looking at your cards. So focused,
I'm not sure you hear; I don't turn my head.
We're in the middle of a game of gin rummy,

when the children show us their hand (or, their parents').
The sun's setting yellow streaks through spruces and pines
that surround us, as we play our game of gin rummy
in the middle of White Mountain National Forest.

Through spruces and pines, sun streaks yellow across my hand,
I scan for four-of-a-kinds, sequences of the same suit.
In the middle of White Mountain National Forest,
my fingers clench my cards; my eyes gaze up,

scan for kin, anyone who looks enough like us—
I'm only half Asian, you said when I met you,
I had already guessed. I too like these children,
I realize—looking and deciding what one is.

You look half Asian, I've been told. A compliment?
I don't know. I hear the children still giggling
as I look back down at my cards, rearrange my kinds and suits.
So evening passes at the campsite—all whispers.

Proof of Language Competency

If I check all the boxes
with the spiral galaxies
and verify
the programmed correct
letters and numbers
into the CAPTCHA
will I
be considered human?
My grandmother calls
and I've forgotten
how to say
in Cantonese: I went for a walk
stopped into
three bookstores
read a book of poems and
I love you too.

Emails from Mom

III.

Subject: Mother's Worst Nightmare

Body: https://www.msn.com/en-us/news/crime/spring-breaker-drugged-raped-and-left
-for-dead-identified-as-24-year-old-philadelphia-woman/ar-BB1eTkXL?li=BBorjTa&ocid
=mailsignout

RE:

I imagine you typing out M-o-t-h-e-r-'-s W-o-r-s-t N-i-g-h-t-m-a-r-e.
All these articles you send me say the same thing; the stories,
though, are not the same. Each girl and their mother suffering
in their own ways. You say you sleep better when I'm at home.
I sleep better after I've watched at least two episodes
of *Law and Order: SVU*. An old obsession as comfort, you know.
In middle school, winter- and summer-break marathons—the TV
permanently set on the ION channel. You'd say *see what bad things
can happen to you*. But I was never afraid: that script felt so far away
from me with you in the other room. Through all the nights I walk home
drunk in the dark, the mornings I run in the woods before dawn,
the years I spend living alone—you're here, just in the other room.
And I promise, I too am just in the other room from you.

IV.

Subject: Happy Sunday!

Body: Have a good day! 😇

RE:

It's Valentine's Day. I received your card in the mail days ago.
It's on my dresser, next to my vermouth. I'm sitting in bed,
working my office job. A purple teddy bear with a pink heart
patched onto its chest stares at me from the closet—your gift
from over a decade ago. Even now, in my late twenties, every
year you give me something—a keychain, blanket, slippers.
Later, I'll put on a velvet skirt just for fun and bake
banana bread. I'll sit on the counter, eat spoonfuls
of it from the loaf pan. You used to leave notes on the counter
for me whenever you left for work before I woke.
Oatmeal's on the stove. Have a good day! Exterminator's
coming at eight. Can you move the clothes to the dryer?
I wish I kept them now—their own kind of valentine.

Something, Not a Love Poem

At midnight I eat your expired *for him* vitamins.

Email with its body as the subject line.

The cut on my thumb from a knife. Or was it paper?

My mom sends me floss in the mail.

The laugh we stained the streets with; the stumbled over sidewalk piss.

The 2-year-old January to-do list in my coat pocket: *order furniture.*

My back bedroom window asks my neighbor for intimacy.

The man I sit next to on the bus tells me he always wanted to marry an Asian woman.

Face ID doesn't recognize me when I cry.

I paid $17.60 in postage and the frame arrived broken.

After the party, you're still the answer to my security questions.

I sleep beside your disassembled bed.

Changed saved address on Google Maps.

I subscribe to the eBird rare bird alert for anywhere but here.

Everything, Everywhere, All at Once

for the movie

In this multiverse, my mom
is still my mom. My dad,
my dad. And my grandma,
still my only living one.
But here she speaks English
and I speak fluent Cantonese—
meaning, she tells me
about her girlhood, curses
her five brothers and my dead
grandpa. I know the nuance of
every slight, the weight
of each complaint. I tell her
about the Chinese poets
I'm reading, the poems
I've written for her.
We go back and forth
some words reserved
for English, others
for Cantonese.
And yet, in this verse
she still reaches for my hand
in the same way,
walking down the street.
She still scrapes the rice
at the bottom of the pot
just for me. My earliest memory
is still my earliest
memory—my small body
sheltered by her small body,
her arms wrapped around me,
my arms hanging off

her shoulders. Still, I remember
her pulling my ears, my head
on her chest as I sleep—
which is to say what's changed
is how we can speak
to one another, but not
how we love.

Return

a sound translation after Jonathan Stalling

grandma I look for you
        gàn mā hei lihk fā yú

follow mother's strength—flower bruise
        faih lóuh má tàih sì gaan haih faai louh bíu sì

barks old horse hoof; time a fast road, mounting silk
        béi yì dá hòi sī hoú fēi tìmh àh? faat séng muhng sìh kèih

to give a coat, open poetry; good ticket, sweet?
        to wake up from a dream period

/////

Hair (once was)

jet black / out of / the womb / full head / of / already labeled / on the / birth certificate / so much / of it / mom said / I've been / picking up / the strands / of your hair / your whole life / once was / grown / just long / enough / to be / bowl cut / by my / aunt's hands / same style / she gave / my brother / once was / pinned up / by a redheaded / hairdresser / at my / best friend's / birthday party / once was / trimmed / in the / elementary / school / bathroom / by a classmate's / curiosity / once was / after Britney / Taylor / Miley / once was never / the photo / from the / internet / I showed / the stylist / once was / partially / highlighted / balayaged / ombred / once was / chest-length / bobbed / but never / pixied / once was / lightened / by the / Arizona / sun and chlorine / once was / red / blue / blonde / violet / and red / again / once was / coiled around / a machine / then curly / once was / cut / by my / own hands / eyes closed / in front / of no mirror / no witness / but myself / to bear / the site / of change / once was / split / at the ends / many times / and again / the ends / rise / to grow / again

At Judy Chicago's Dinner Party

The way to arrive is up and winding, through rooms and rooms until *the* room is met. A corner entrance. The air changes, the light changes—all signaling something sacred. I walk around and around again. The women are represented on *39 fourteen-inch China-painted porcelain plates*. There are no East Asian women here. On *The Heritage Floor*, there are names painted in cursive: *999 mythical and historical women of achievement, who were selected to contextualize the 39 women represented in the place settings*. They make up the base of the table— porcelain tiles. *Each tile was hand-cast and hand-sanded at the China Boutique outside of Los Angeles*. A list of names can be found on a Wikipedia page, in a table with five columns—name, birthdate, location, group (related place setting), notes. There are no East Asian women here.

My Mother in My House

peels oranges. My mother in my house
wipes dirt off edges of wall molding.
My mother in my house rearranges
the linen closet. My mother in my house
showers. My mother in my house checks
the best-by dates on Greek yogurt in the fridge
and asks *why don't you have any blinds?*
My mother in my house takes photos
of photos of my beloved. My mother
in my house pronounces quinoa like *qi-wah*,
and scrolls the facebook group she's joined
for reviews of new products at Trader Joe's.
My mother in my house before she goes
leaves peeled oranges on the table, every time.

Girl Wrapped in Bitter Gourd Vine

after Saeed Jones

Granddaughter who is no one,
        granddaughter who is yet to come—

amidst these rows sowed
        with seeds of bitter gourd,

I stick to centuries-old superstition.

See how my eyes become milk
        for you? Baskets of fruits & fake money

delivered to all your ancestors' graves.

Call me and I'm at your side,
        one incense burning

behind my ear. Ask me
        and I'll make sure

you're the best fed, with chicken—
        good luck pecking at your feet.

Hold nothing but palms pressed

together and bow three times
        into the smoke.

Hair (variations)

i.

permanent wave

hair
      sectioned
            wound
tight around
      each rod
turned
      outward,
inward,
      and again
            each strand
      slithers
waits for
      a threshold
of permanence

ii.
at-home dye

hair pressed
      over
         foils brushed
        on bleach
      made
            to strip brown
      away, rust

color remains
        still lighter, still
        better
                for dyeing
        electric
        blue by my
own hand
        splat brand
i massage
        the color
        onto each
strand, let
it set
        for hours walk
                around
        the house, my hair
                wrapped
in foil in
        plastic
to prevent
staining

   iii.

    self-cut

        hair parted
front section
        pulled
over eyes, scissors
                held
up above
        eyebrows
it's not
        precision i

am trying for
                    but
          immediate
          change, a face
that might
                    surprise me
for a few days
          when i look
in the mirror
          trimmings
          on my cheeks i
blow
          them away

Granddaughter

a sound translation after Jonathan Stalling

néih faai fàan-heui ngūk-kéi gin ngin ngin
       neither faithful—looking, gleaning

mh haih jùng saht—wán, got wòh
       my high young sat wan, gut woe—

ngóh gòu hauh sāang chóh behng, du sauh fú
       augur housing. jar being, too sorrowful.

sàhn sing ngūk. chihng chyùhn joih, bai ngai.

Where I Find Her / Where I Leave Her

Strands of my hair collect dust
at the corners of the bathroom

that my mother has not yet
stepped into, not yet kneeled

onto the cold, white tile
to pick up what I've shed.

I once shaved her back
in another bathroom where

she may be standing right now.
Where she may be looking

at the photo of us tucked between
glass and wood frame. Where I see

her tray of perfumes reflected
against my torso, in my mirror

even though it is not here.
Even when she is not here

her hand reaches out
to brush my hair.

Lightwell

for the Wing Luke Museum

Inside an interior apartment
of the old East Kong Yick Building,
the tour guide explains how
a regulation forced windows
into these rooms—otherwise
buried within the labyrinth
of walls and hallways—sections
of which were bulldozed to make
this aspirational alley
we are looking out at.
They call it a lightwell.

Each room back then shared
between three to four men,
one bed made possible
by shift work—one hand
replacing another on the handle
of the machine or hoe. One
body lying in the impression
of another on the sunken
mattress—sheets worn and
browned, the details now preserved.

I walk toward the window,
which looks over to a window
on the other side, another interior
apartment. Two sides of an interior
don't make an exterior, I think

to myself—who opened
these windows? What hands lifted
this weight up? I can't know—
but it's a sunny day in Seattle,
and there's light in this space between.

Hair (now has)

not been cut / dyed / curled / straightened / brushed in _____ years / hours / days / still / that whisper / of once was

A Tattoo for My Mother

Do not pluck your eyebrows—my mother's warning:
they'd never grow back. At 17, she took the tweezers to her skin
until there was no hair left. She was determined
to remake them into the perfect shape. For decades she outlined
the just-right arc, until she decided she'd brave the needle
and get them tattooed—finally, erase her mistake.

I held her hand throughout, and checked for any mistakes.
There were none, thus no need to give warning
to her coworker who wanted the same, but was afraid of the needle.
You won't feel a thing—just a little prick on the skin.
For weeks afterwards, she stood before the mirror outlining
with her finger the perfect shape made permanent. I was determined

to have my own mark of permanence. The needle didn't deter me
either, from getting my own tattoo. She said it would be a mistake
but I was already using calculus class to sketch outlines
of floral designs, phrases I loved. I looked up the warnings,
scrolled through tattoos gone wrong—and still wanted to mark my skin.
I found a place that did not check IDs, and sanitized their needles.

I wanted beauty, some proof that I didn't need her—
my mother—to hold my hand. I was determined
to be my own person; control my body, my skin.
I told her I was old enough to make my own mistakes.
And yet, to this day she emails me articles—headlines a warning:
"Woman attacked on her morning run." My mother outlining

the endless ways I could die. Her voice in my head will outlive
her. Since I was young, she's prepared me not to need her;
showed me the binder I'd need in case she went without warning,
I was to call her lawyer. Everything had already been determined—
my mother, an accountant, sorting assets makes no mistakes.
She says: *I'm leaving it all to you and your brother, my kin.*

These days I don't see her very much—when I do, I notice her skin
wrinkled in new places—compounded worries, she could outline
the thoughts that have kept her up: worst fears, my mistakes.
Though she's prepared me not to, she wants me to need her—
to be the one I call at 3am in crisis. She's determined
to quell those little disasters that come without warning.

She's always there, waiting to say *it's okay*. And, *didn't I warn you?*
My mistakes: that tattoo I got or other bad thing I did, undeterred,
outlining my own story—this paper, my skin. My needle—this pen.

Spring Reflection

       You crave
For the wheels to ride across the puddle, muddied
With pebbles & all your past lives too

       You want to find again
That sky blue that's been shut tight
All winter long

       You don't know why
When you finally do
The birds mistake each strand of your hair for a branch

       You wish for the pecking to stop
For the stillness of a bud before blossom
To return to you

       You ask for a taste
Of the warm cold wind on your wet lips
Just once more—

       You try to remember
What everything was like before
But you take a sip from the teacup filled with pollen
       & ash, instead

Acknowledgments

"My Name" contains a line from *Romeo and Juliet*. The italicized text in "Portrait of Louisa Cobb Thompson by an Unidentified Chinese" is from a museum didactic at the Nantucket Whaling Museum. The italicized text in "At Judy Chicago's Dinner Party" is from the Brooklyn Museum's web page about *The Dinner Party*. "Autumn Thoughts" takes its title and inspiration from Tu Fu and Meng Chiao. "Diaspora," "Return," and "Granddaughter" are inspired by Jonathan Stalling's *Yingelishi* process (though not completely loyal to it) and consult Parker Po-fei Huang's *Cantonese Dictionary* for translations.

Thank you to the following sources and texts for their invaluable help in and/or inspiration for the beast that "American | Ghost | Chestnut" became: Haven Metcalf's 1914 article in the *Journal of Heredity*, "The Chestnut Bark Disease: An Undesirable Immigrant Which Has Secured Firm Foothold in Eastern United States—Breeding Resistant Species Probably the Only Solution of Problem—Opportunity for Orchardists On Pacific Coast to Build Up Industry"; The American Chestnut Foundation's *Mighty Giants: An American Chestnut Anthology*; various late nineteenth and early twentieth century news articles regarding the chestnut blight and the "Chinese question" from the Library of Congress's Chronicling America archive; the Library of Congress's Immigration and Relocation in US History (Chinese) archive; Anne Anlin Cheng's *Ornamentalism*; Jack London's "The Unparalleled Invasion"; Lisa Lowe's *Immigrant Acts*; Anna Tsing's *The Mushroom at the End of the World*. The crown sonnet form is indebted to Marilyn Nelson. The crossword was made on crosswordlabs.com—you can find and solve it online by visiting the site and searching "X-bred."

Thank you to the following journals and editors who believed in and published versions of these poems: *Bellevue Literary Review* ("Speech Derapy"); *Blackbird* ("Portrait of Louisa Cobb Thompson," "Poem Written in My Grandmother's Dress"); *Breakwater Review* ("Girl Wrapped in Bitter Gourd Vine"); *Copper Nickel* ("Lipogram"); *Electric Literature* ("Something, Not a Love Poem"); *Ghost City Review* ("Two-Winged Sunset in Penang"); *Minola Review* ("Proof of Language Competency"); *New Ohio Review* ("Spring Reflection"); *[PANK]* ("So Many Wet Feet Everywhere"); *Poetry Online* ("The Leng³est Neoi⁵⁻²"); *Rhino* ("Hair [once was]"); *Sonora Review* ("Open Wide"); *Sundog Lit* ("Where I Find Her / Where I Leave Her"); *Tupelo Quarterly* ("A Tattoo for My Mother"); *Worcester Review* ("My Mother in My House").

With Gratitude and Love—

To you, reader. It will always be unbelievable to me that you are here.

To my family and my ancestors. To my mom, who slips Band-Aids into my purse, and my dad, who moves me from one part of the country to another, and another. To my grandparents, who will never read this book but who made it.

To my teachers: Mrs. Duerbig, Mrs. Gordon, Mrs. Breitwieser, Mrs. Auble, Mr. Small, Mr. Showman, Mrs. Burgess, Mrs. Thomas.

To my professors at the University of Arizona and the University of Utah: Patrick Baliani, John Paul Hurh, Jennifer Jenkins, Matthew Abraham, Crystal Rudds, Angela Marie Smith, David Roh, Lindsey Drager, Michael Mejia, Lance Olsen, Douglas Kearney, Kate Coles, and Jacqueline Osherow.

To Joshua Marie Wilkinson—for believing in my voice.

To the places and spaces where this book was lived and drafted—from Cleveland to Malaysia to India to Massachusetts to Salt Lake City, and all the crevices in between, it's been a true adventure.

To the Taft-Nicholson Center—for the hummingbirds and huckleberries.

To Mike Foley and David Nader, for being the best sustainability department in the world.

To my mentors and friends, for the nourishment—Chet Phillips, Lysette Davi, Jill Burchell, Emily Kotay, Laura Gronewold, Sharon Overstreet, Karna Walter, Crystal Soltero, David Scott Allen, Lara Buluç, Paul Wetzel, Levonne Tran, Madeline Kiser, Alanna Gerardi, Fiona Davey, Trishna Desai, Saba Keramati, Jacob Winkelman, Obum Ugbor, Amy Raiff, Julie Mobilian, Natalie Welch, Levonne Tran, Joshua Mora, Julie Palmer, Trevor Ledbetter, Cole Pihl, Mal Labriola, Ian Petty, Evan Amadu, Jaimie Choi, Natalie Slater.

To every person I met while traveling from April to November 2019—you touched my life in ways that made this book possible.

To the Fine Arts Work Center—for the summer workshop scholarship and community. And, for the time as a bedfellow!

To my Bread Loaf Environmental Writers' Conference—for reading very early chestnut poems! And for suggesting I make it into a crown sonnet. To the Rona Jaffe Foundation for the opportunity. Thank you for the community.

To my peers and friends at the University of Utah: Chengru He, Jasmine Khaliq, Erin O'Luanaigh, Jess Tanck, Jamie Smith, Allie Field Bell, Ali Myers, Nick Pierce, Corley Miller—for collectively surviving Jackie's workshop and reading the very first draft of this manuscript.

Endless thanks for holding and shaping so many of the poems in here. To Audrey Bauman, Abbey Corcoran, Michael Farfel, Brandon Young, Matty Glasgow, Daniel Uncapher, Jacob Yordy, Garrett Biggs, Lindsey Webb, Alleliah Nuguid, Max Schleicher, Karli Sam, Aristotle Johns—for the good company.

To my students—for all your insight and delight.

To the Asian American writers who made, and continue to make, this work possible for me—Maxine Hong Kingston, Carlos Bulosan, Theresa Hak Kyung Cha, Cynthia Kadohata, Li-Young Lee, Marilyn Chin—and too many more to list. Thank you, thank you.

To *Law & Order: SVU*, matcha lattes, chocolate cake, whiskey, Mason's Creamery, The Happy Dog, Grey Matter Books, Tulie Bakery, Trader Joe's, Purgatory Bar—for getting me through.

To Brenda Shaughnessy and everyone at the University of Iowa Press for putting this book into the world. It's been a dream—thank you so much.

To my colleagues and community at Sewanee—for opening the door.

To Paisley Rekdal—this book would simply not be what it is without your attention, hard questions, and critical insight.

To Jordan Callahan Lopez—for every joy and heartbreak you've laughed through with me. For being my first reader and best cheerleader. From The Happy Dog basement to here—cheers, bb.

To Samyak Shertok—for the other side. Danyabad.

Iowa Poetry Prize and Edwin Ford Piper Poetry Award Winners

1987
Elton Glaser, *Tropical Depressions*
Michael Pettit, *Cardinal Points*

1988
Bill Knott, *Outremer*
Mary Ruefle, *The Adamant*

1989
Conrad Hilberry, *Sorting the Smoke*
Terese Svoboda, *Laughing Africa*

1990
Philip Dacey, *Night Shift at the Crucifix Factory*
Lynda Hull, *Star Ledger*

1991
Greg Pape, *Sunflower Facing the Sun*
Walter Pavlich, *Running near
the End of the World*

1992
Lola Haskins, *Hunger*
Katherine Soniat, *A Shared Life*

1993
Tom Andrews, *The Hemophiliac's Motorcycle*
Michael Heffernan, *Love's Answer*
John Wood, *In Primary Light*

1994
James McKean, *Tree of Heaven*
Bin Ramke, *Massacre of the Innocents*
Ed Roberson, *Voices Cast Out to Talk Us In*

1995
Ralph Burns, *Swamp Candles*
Maureen Seaton, *Furious Cooking*

1996
Pamela Alexander, *Inland*
Gary Gildner, *The Bunker in the Parsley Fields*
John Wood, *The Gates of the Elect Kingdom*

1997
Brendan Galvin, *Hotel Malabar*
Leslie Ullman, *Slow Work through Sand*

1998
Kathleen Peirce, *The Oval Hour*
Bin Ramke, *Wake*
Cole Swensen, *Try*

1999
Larissa Szporluk, *Isolato*
Liz Waldner, *A Point Is That Which Has No Part*

2000
Mary Leader, *The Penultimate Suitor*

2001
Joanna Goodman, *Trace of One*
Karen Volkman, *Spar*

2002
Lesle Lewis, *Small Boat*
Peter Jay Shippy, *Thieves' Latin*

2003
Michele Glazer, *Aggregate of Disturbances*
Dainis Hazners, *(some of) The Adventures of Carlyle, My Imaginary Friend*

2004
Megan Johnson, *The Waiting*
Susan Wheeler, *Ledger*

2005
Emily Rosko, *Raw Goods Inventory*
Joshua Marie Wilkinson, *Lug Your Careless Body out of the Careful Dusk*

2006
Elizabeth Hughey, *Sunday Houses the Sunday House*
Sarah Vap, *American Spikenard*

2008
Andrew Michael Roberts, *something has to happen next*
Zach Savich, *Full Catastrophe Living*

2009
Samuel Amadon, *Like a Sea*
Molly Brodak, *A Little Middle of the Night*

2010
Julie Hanson, *Unbeknownst*
L. S. Klatt, *Cloud of Ink*

2011
Joseph Campana, *Natural Selections*
Kerri Webster, *Grand & Arsenal*

2012
Stephanie Pippin, *The Messenger*

2013
Eric Linsker, *La Far*
Alexandria Peary, *Control Bird Alt Delete*

2014
JoEllen Kwiatek, *Study for Necessity*

2015
John Blair, *Playful Song Called Beautiful*
Lindsay Tigue, *System of Ghosts*

2016
Adam Giannelli, *Tremulous Hinge*
Timothy Daniel Welch, *Odd Bloom Seen from Space*

2017
Alicia Mountain, *High Ground Coward*
Lisa Wells, *The Fix*

2018
Cassie Donish, *The Year of the Femme*
Rob Schlegel, *In the Tree Where the Double Sex Sleeps*

2019
William Fargason, *Love Song to the Demon-Possessed Pigs of Gadara*
Jennifer Habel, *The Book of Jane*

2020
Emily Pittinos, *The Last Unkillable Thing*
Felicia Zamora, *I Always Carry My Bones*

2021
Emily Pérez, *What Flies Want*

2022
Melissa Crowe, *Lo*
Maggie Queeney, *In Kind*

2023
Stephanie Choi, *The Lengest Neoi*
Peter Mishler, *Children in Tactical Gear*